Belinda Jeffery's

asian
perfection

COOKING CLASS

asian
perfection

HINKLER BOOKS

asian
perfection

Food Editor
Ellen Argyriou

Creative Director
Sam Grimmer

Project Editor
Lara Morcombe

HB
HINKLER
BOOKS

First published in 2004 by Hinkler Books Pty Ltd
17–23 Redwood Drive
Dingley, VIC 3172 Australia
www.hinklerbooks.com
Reprinted.2004

ISBN 1741215838
EAN 9781741215830

Printed and bound in China

contents

an introduction to asian cooking

The largest continent on earth, Asia is home to an exciting and diverse range of cuisines. In Western countries Chinese, Japanese, Indian, Thai and Vietnamese food outlets have been a welcome addition to the restaurant scene. The popularity of Asian food has grown immeasurably and with it a desire to make this cuisine part of home-cooked family meals. Supermarkets now stock a considerable range of the necessary Asian ingredients, both grocery lines and fresh Asian vegetables, herbs and flavorings. This book will help you to prepare a healthy Asian meal, packed full of flavor.

stocking the pantry

The following guide will assist you to select a basic supply.

sauces

Listed are the most widely used Asian sauces – it is essential to stock 2–3 of these in your pantry.

soy sauce: A thin brown sauce made from soy beans, wheat, yeast and salt. It is aged and distilled to make the sauce. It is widely used in Asian cooking. Light soy sauce is light in color and density and will flavor foods without adding color. Dark soy sauce is darker, thicker and richer in flavor as it is aged longer than the light soy. It gives a rich brown color to the food. Indonesian soy or kecap manis is thick, dark and sweet. For a similar result use dark soy sauce and add brown sugar. All soy sauces will keep indefinitely on the pantry shelf.

oyster sauce: This sauce is made by fermenting dried oysters with soy sauce and brine. It adds a rich savory flavor to meat and vegetable dishes and is also used in stir-fries. Be sure to store it in the refrigerator after opening.

hoisin sauce: Hoisin is made from fermented soya beans, garlic, chilli and spices. Sweet and spicy in flavor it is used as a condiment or to add to pork, chicken or beef dishes. It can be interchanged with oyster sauce in recipes, and can be stored on a pantry shelf.

chilli sauce: Various varieties are available. Choose one to suit your tastes. Chinese sweet chilli sauce is a hot sweet and sour sauce. It is added in small quantities to fish dishes and stir-fries. Thai chilli sauce or náam phrík is used mainly as a table condiment. Some are hot and strong, flavored with shrimp paste and fish sauce. Milder varieties are available and are used as a dipping sauce. Store these sauces in the refrigerator after opening.

fish sauce: An important ingredient in Southeast Asian cuisine. A little added to the cooking has a major impact on flavor. It is made from fermented whitebait and salt. Fish sauce adds a pungent flavor to dipping sauces, soups, stir-fries, rice, noodles and salad dressings. It can be stored on a pantry shelf.

black bean sauce: Made from fermented black soya beans, chilli and spices. Used in stir-fry meat, or mixed stir-fries. Hot bean or sweet bean sauce is available. It should be stored in the refrigerator after opening.

shrimp sauce: Much like fish sauce but made with small shrimps or prawns and brine. It resembles anchovy paste, which is often used as a substitute. It can be stored on the pantry shelf.

spices, curry and other flavoring agents

five-spice powder: A very popular spice in Chinese cookery. It is a ground mixture of anise, pepper, star anise, cloves, cinnamon and fennel.

turmeric: A plant root that has been dried and powdered. It gives a mild flavor but is prized for the color it gives to food, particularly rice. It is included in curry powder mixes for that purpose.

cumin: An essential ingredient in prepared curry powder mixes. It has a delightful fragrance and goes well with beef and lamb.

dried coriander seed or ground coriander: The dried seeds of the fresh coriander plant. It gives a delightful fragrance to food.

tamarind liquid: Tamarind liquid is an important flavoring agent in Indian, Indonesian and Malayan cooking. The long fibers of the tamarind pod are soaked in water to extract the flavor, the pulp is discarded and the liquid is used. Dried tamarind pulp is sold in packets. There is also a bottled tamarind liquid available, perhaps not as good as soaking the pulp to make the liquid.

curry: Curry is the word that refers to the sauce around braised meat and chicken. The

spice mixes used to make curry in India and Southeast Asia are individually blended according to the fragrance and strength of heat desired. For convenience curry powder (a ready mix blend of spices for the sauce) became commercially available a long time ago. The blends now cater to a wider range of tastes. Curry pastes, which are spice blends roasted in oil, represent particular spice blends, eg, Thai red or green curry paste and rendang curry paste. In your pantry, stock a mild and fragrant curry powder or paste. If a hotter taste is required, add a little chilli powder. Store dry powders on the pantry shelf and curry pastes in the refrigerator after opening

dried shrimps: A little dried shrimp is used to give a delightful flavor to food. Soak as directed and store in a tightly closed jar on a pantry shelf.

white miso: Important in Japanese cuisine, it's used to flavor stocks and soups. It is made from yellow soya beans, boiled and crushed, then allowed to ferment. It should be stored in the refrigerator.

rice wine: A wine made from rice. Mirin, a sweet rice wine, is also used.

dry and sweet sherry: sIf you are fond of Chinese cooking, a bottle of either is useful in your pantry.

rice vinegar: Rice vinegar is clear to pale gold in color, with a mildly sweet flavor. It's used in dipping sauces and salad dressings. A little sweet sherry may be substituted.

palm sugar: Palm sugar is obtained from the sap of the coconut and palmyra palm trees. It has a strong sweet flavor. Dark brown sugar is a good substitute.

rice and dried noodles

Rice and dried noodles are the staples of Asian cuisine and you should always have a cache readily available in your pantry.

short-grain or medium-grain rice: These varieties are used mainly with Chinese cooking.

jasmine and basmati: Both are a long-grain rice and are preferred with Indian and Malaysian dishes.

glutinous rice: Also known as sticky rice, this rice is used mainly in sweet dishes. It clings together when cooked and blends well with sugar and coconut milk.

dried rice noodles: Also known as rice sticks or rice vermicelli, soak dried rice noodles in hot water until soft, drain well and use in stir-fries or soups. When deep-fried in their dried state they puff up to a crunchy texture to use in salads or to top a stir-fry.

bean thread noodles: Made from mung bean starch, bean thread noodles are also known

as cellophane noodles. Soak in hot water before use, drain and use in stir-fries, soups or salads.

wheat noodles: Available in various widths and either plain or enriched with egg, wheat noodles need to be boiled and drained well before inclusion in a dish.

Supermarkets stock a large range of instant noodles or quick cooking noodles. Some include a flavor sachet. They can be added to a quick stir-fry after cooking as directed on the pack.

fresh asian ingredients

Fresh flavoring ingredients are important in Asian cooking.

garlic: For a mild flavor, fry slices of garlic in the oil then remove before the addition of other ingredients. A more defined flavor is achieved if garlic is minced and included with the other ingredients. Use fresh garlic. Garlic cloves are best stored in a jar in the refrigerator.

ginger: Ginger is an essential flavoring ingredient. Cut a 1–2 cm piece from the ginger root. Peel thinly and slice very finely or grate. Any remaining ginger root may be wrapped in damp paper, placed in a plastic bag and stored in the refrigerator crisper for 2–3 weeks.

lemon grass: This imparts a characteristic sour flavor to Asian dishes. Trim away the outer blades and cut the white bulbous part into thin slices or chop finely. Lemon grass will keep in the refrigerator crisper for up to 2 months.

chillies: Small, red, hot chillies must be handled with care. If an intense hot flavor is needed, chop the chilli with the seeds and vein. If a milder heat is desired, split the chilli and remove the seeds and thick vein. The hot part of the chilli is concentrated in the seeds and vein, and will remain on your fingers. If, after handling chillies, you touch your tongue, lips or eyes, severe irritation will result. Wash your hands immediately after handling chillies or wear rubber gloves.

coconut milk and cream: Is made from fresh, grated coconut 'meat'. Canned coconut milk is available as either thin or thick. Thin coconut milk is used for long simmering with other ingredients. Thick coconut milk or cream is added at the end of the recipe to give flavor and a smooth consistency. Store left over coconut milk or cream in a sealed container in the refrigerator for up to 1 week. It may also be frozen for longer storage, but loses some of its smooth texture.

fresh noodles: A wide variety may be found in the refrigerator cabinets at supermarkets as well as in Asian food stores. Varieties include Hokkien noodles and the thinner Singapore noodles, both made from wheat flour. Rice noodles include the Japanese udon and the flat pad thai, which are gluten free.

meat: Many Asian recipes call for thinly sliced meat, particularly for a stir-fry. Always cut the meat across the grain for a tender result. Purchase the meat in a thick piece or 'nut' not a slice, to be able to cut across the grain. For thinly sliced meat, freeze the meat for 2 hours to keep it firm under the blade of the knife. Trays of stir-fry strips or small cubed meats are available in butcher shops and supermarkets.

wrappers: These are squares of noodle dough used to wrap food in to make spring rolls and wontons. Both rice and wheat-based wrappers are available. They can be found in the refrigerator cabinets at supermarkets and Asian food stores.

soups
salads
and
appetizers

thai fish sticks with cucumber salad

ingredients

salad
1 cucumber, peeled and thinly sliced
4 tablespoons white-wine vinegar
4 tablespoons white sugar
1 large red or green chilli, deseeded
  and finely chopped
1 small green onion, thinly sliced

fish sticks
small handful cilantro
4 green onions, chopped
450 g (14 oz) cod or other skinless
  white fish fillet, cubed
3 tablespoons red curry paste
1 teaspoon salt
2 teaspoons lime juice
1 large egg white
12 stalks lemon grass

serves 4

i

preparation time
25 minutes

cooking time
6 minutes

nutritional value
per serve
fat: 2.6 g
carbohydrate: 8.3 g
protein: 9.4 g

1 Combine cucumber, vinegar, sugar, chilli and 1 small green onion with 4 tablespoons of cold water. Cover and set aside in a cool place.

2 Place cilantro and remaining green onions in a food processor and process until finely chopped. Add fish, curry paste, salt and lime juice and process until the fish is finely chopped. Add egg white and continue processing until the mixture is stiff.

3 Divide the fish mixture into 12 portions, then carefully press each around a lemon grass stick, forming a 'sausage' shape. Preheat the broiler to high. Place the fish sticks on a lightly oiled baking sheet and broil for 6 minutes, turning once, until cooked and lightly browned on all sides. Serve with the cucumber salad.

japanese jumbo shrimp and vegetable tempura

ingredients

1 small zucchini
salt
4 green jumbo shrimp
1 red bell pepper
1 large egg
150 g (5 oz) all purpose flour
1/2 cup (125 ml, 4 fl oz) ice-cold water
peanut oil for deep-frying
lime wedges to serve
soy sauce to serve
serves 4

i

preparation time
25 minutes, plus
20 minutes
standing

cooking time
10 minutes

**nutritional value
per serve**
fat: 1.4 g
carbohydrate: 19 g
protein: 7.2 g

1 Cut the zucchini in half across the center, trim the end and cut each half lengthways into 4. Sprinkle with salt and set aside for 20 minutes. Shell the shrimp, leaving tails attached. Devein, using a sharp knife. Rinse and refrigerate. Deseed the bell pepper and cut into 8 strips.

2 Break the egg into a mixing bowl. Mix in the ice-cold water and fold in the flour to make a lumpy batter.

3 Heat 5 cm of oil in a wok or skillet. Coat the zucchini slices in batter and deep-fry for 3 minutes or until golden,

turning halfway through. Drain on kitchen paper and keep warm. Repeat with bell pepper strips. Coat shrimp and cook for 1 minute. Serve immediately with lime wedges and soy sauce.

1 Into a large bowl, place chickpea flour, ground rice, baking soda, chilli powder, turmeric, curry powder and salt. Gradually add water, stirring constantly until smooth. Add green onions, zucchini and eggplant and combine well.

2 Pour the oil into a wok to a depth of 2 inches and heat over a medium to high heat. Check oil is hot enough by dropping in a small piece of vegetable – it should sizzle. Gently drop heaping tablespoons of mixture, 4 at a time, into the hot oil and fry for 2–3 minutes until golden. Turn over and cook for a further 2–3 minutes until crisp. Remove with a slotted spoon and drain on paper towels. Serve with mint and cucumber raita. Recipe opposite.

vegetable bhajis

ingredients

10 green onions, finely chopped
2 small zucchinis, coarsely grated
1 eggplant, finely diced
vegetable oil for frying

batter
100 g (3$^1/_2$ oz) chickpea flour
50 g (2 oz) ground rice
$^1/_4$ teaspoon baking soda
1 teaspoon chilli powder
1 teaspoon turmeric
1-2 tablespoons mild or hot curry powder
1 teaspoon salt
225 ml (7$^1/_2$ fl oz) water

serves 4

i

preparation time
25 minutes

cooking time
30 minutes

nutritional value per serve
fat: 0.5 g
carbohydrate: 13 g
protein: 2.5 g

cucumber and mint raita

hour. Drain through a strainer, pressing out as much liquid as possible. Dry in 2 layers of absorbent paper.

2 In a clean bowl, place cucumbers and toss in mint.

3 In another bowl, combine garlic, ginger, yogurt and lemon juice. Add to the cucumbers and toss well to combine. Refrigerate for 1 hour. Serve with the vegetable bhajis or to accompany a curry dish.

preparation time
10 minutes, plus
1 hour standing
and 1 hour
refrigeration

nutritional value per serve
fat: 1.8 g
carbohydrate: 4 g
protein: 2.6 g

ingredients

2 large cucumbers
2 teaspoons salt
2 tablespoons fresh mint leaves, chopped
1 small clove garlic, minced
1/4 teaspoon finely grated fresh ginger
1 cup (250 ml, 8 fl oz) natural yogurt
2 teaspoons lemon juice
serves 4

1 Peel cucumbers and slice very thinly. Place in a bowl and sprinkle with salt, toss to mix salt through. Stand for 1

spring rolls

ingredients

20 g (²/₃ oz) vermicelli
3 tablespoons vegetable oil
3 cloves garlic, finely chopped
310 g (10 oz) minced chicken
¼ cabbage, cut into fine strips
1 carrot, cut into thin strips
2 green onions,
   finely chopped
½ teaspoon salt
1 teaspoon sugar
½ teaspoon white pepper
1 tablespoon oyster sauce
20-25 rice paper wrappers
1 egg, beaten
extra oil for deep frying
lettuce and mint leaves to serve
makes 20

1 Soak vermicelli in hot water for 5 minutes until soft. Drain, cut into 2 inches lengths and set aside.

i

preparation time
15 minutes

cooking time
15 minutes

nutritional value
per serve
fat: 9.2 g
carbohydrate: 5 g
protein: 9.8 g

2 Heat 3 tablespoons oil in a wok or skillet, add garlic and chicken and cook for 8 minutes, stirring constantly until crumbly. Add cabbage, carrot, green onions and vermicelli. Cook on high for about 3 minutes until vegetables soften.

3 Turn off heat. Add salt, sugar, pepper and oyster sauce, stir to mix well and allow to cool. Brush each side of the rice wrappers with water. Place 1 tablespoon of mixture onto each wrapper, turn sides in first, roll and seal each with beaten egg. Refrigerate until needed.

4 Heat extra oil in wok or skillet. Deep-fry a few rolls at a time until golden. Drain on absorbent paper. Serve on lettuce leaves garnished with mint. Serve with your favorite sweet chilli or plum sauce.

steamed stuffed cucumbers

ingredients

500 g (1 lb) cucumbers
375g (12 oz) can water chestnuts,
 drained and finely chopped
2¹/₂ tablespoons glutinous rice flour
sesame oil
¹/₂ teaspoon salt
¹/₂ teaspoon sugar
1 small carrot, peeled and finely diced
4 black dried mushrooms, soaked,
 drained and finely chopped
³/₄ cup (185 ml, 6 fl oz) water
1¹/₂ teaspoons cornstarch
serves 4–6

1 Thinly peel cucumbers and cut into 1/2 inch thick slices. Scoop out seeds with a teaspoon leaving a base layer. Place cucumber shells in boiling water for 1 minute. Rinse in cold water, drain and dust inside with a little cornstarch.

2 In a bowl, place finely diced water chestnuts, glutinous rice flour, sesame oil and half the salt and sugar. Add carrot and mushrooms and mix well. Pile high into the cucumber circles. Place circles on a plate and set on steaming rack over hot water in a wok. Cover and steam for 15–20 minutes.

3 Place a drop of sesame oil, the remaining salt and sugar and the water into a small saucepan and bring to the boil. Blend the cornstarch with a little water, add to the saucepan and stir until liquid boils and thickens. Cool to warm. Spoon over each steamed cucumber ring to glaze. Allow to cool. Serve at room temperature.

preparation time
15 minutes
cooking time
15 minutes

nutritional value per serve
fat: 1.7 g
carbohydrate: 7 g
protein: 0.8 g

balinese chicken satay

ingredients

1 stalk lemon grass
1 onion, chopped
1 clove garlic, minced
2 teaspoons ground cilantro
1 teaspoon turmeric
juice of 1/2 lemon
1 teaspoon salt
3 chicken breast fillets, cut into 1/2 inch cubes
1/2 cucumber, pared into ribbons with a vegetable peeler, to serve

satay sauce

1 small onion, chopped
1 clove garlic, minced
1 tablespoon peanut oil
1 teaspoon chilli powder
155 ml (5 fl oz) can coconut milk
75 g (2 1/2 oz) roasted salted peanuts, finely ground
1 tablespoon soft dark brown sugar
1 tablespoon fresh lemon juice

serves 4

2 Place the chicken in a non-metallic bowl and coat with the paste. Cover and marinate in the refrigerator for 2 hours, or overnight. If using wooden skewers, soak them in water for 10 minutes.

3 To make the satay sauce, process the onion and garlic to a paste in a food processor. Heat the oil in a heavy-bottomed saucepan and fry the paste for 5 minutes, stirring. Mix in the chilli powder, then the remaining sauce ingredients. Bring to the boil, stirring, then simmer for 10 minutes.

1 Peel the outer layer from the lemon grass and chop the lower white bulbous part, discarding the fibrous top. Process to a paste with the onion, garlic, coriander, turmeric, lemon juice and 1 teaspoon of salt in a food processor.

4 Preheat the broiler to high. Thread the chicken onto 8 skewers. Broil for 10 minutes, turning once, until cooked. Serve with the cucumber ribbons and satay sauce.

i

preparation time
30 minutes, plus 2 hours marinating

cooking time
25 minutes

nutritional value per serve
fat: 12.9 g
carbohydrate: 4 g
protein: 8.9 g

vietnamese herb salad rolls with peanut sauce

ingredients

55 g (2 oz) cellophane noodles
3 tablespoons rice vinegar
1 tablespoon fish sauce
4 tablespoons roasted peanuts, crushed
12 jumbo cooked shrimp, finely chopped
20 thai basil leaves, finely sliced
10 asian mint leaves, finely sliced
a handful cilantro, finely chopped
4 leaves bok choy (pak choi), finely shredded
2 cabbage leaves, very finely shredded
5 green onions, finely sliced lengthwise
1 medium carrot, grated
1 packet 8 inch square rice paper wrappers

sauce

2 tablespoons peanut oil
5 cloves garlic, minced
1/2 small red chilli pepper, minced
5 tablespoons peanut butter
1 1/2 tablespoons tomato paste
3 tablespoons hoi sin sauce
1 teaspoon sugar
1 teaspoon fish sauce
3/4 cup (185 ml, 6 fl oz) water
40 g (1 1/4 oz) peanuts, crushed

makes 16–20

1 In a bowl of hot water, soak the cellophane noodles for 5–10 minutes until tender, drain immediately and rinse with

cold water. Cut noodles with scissors to a manageable length. In a large bowl, toss noodles with vinegar, fish sauce, roasted peanuts and shrimp. Add the prepared fresh herbs, bok choy, cabbage, green onions and carrot. Toss well.

2 Working with 1 wrapper at a time, soak the rice wrapper in warm water for 30 seconds and lie on a flat surface. Place a heaping tablespoon of filling on the wrapper about 1 inch in from front edge and sides. Fold front edge over the filling, fold in the side edges and roll up. Repeat with the remaining ingredients.

3 Heat the oil in a saucepan and sauté the garlic and minced chilli for about 2 minutes until softened. Add all remaining sauce ingredients and beat while heating. Bring to the boil and simmer about 3 minutes until thickened slightly. To serve, slice each roll on the diagonal, then rest one half over the other. Serve the sauce separately in a small pot for dipping.

i

preparation time
20 minutes

cooking time
10 minutes

nutritional value
per serve
fat: 9.8 g
carbohydrate: 7.1 g
protein: 13.6 g

leek, lime and coconut soup

ingredients

2 tablespoons olive oil
3 leeks, thinly sliced
1 green chilli pepper, deseeded and
chopped
2 potatoes, diced
grated zest and juice of 2 limes
salt and black pepper
600 ml (1 pint) vegetable stock
225 ml (7½ fl oz) can coconut milk
cilantro to garnish
extra lime slices to garnish
serves 4

1 In a large heavy-bottomed saucepan, heat the oil and add the leeks, chilli, potatoes, lime zest and seasoning. Cook for 2 minutes, add stock and bring to the boil. Reduce the heat and simmer for 20–25 minutes, until the potatoes are tender. Leave to cool slightly.

2 In a food processor, blend soup briefly to make a chunky, creamy mixture. Return soup to the pan.

3 Stir in the lime juice, then add the coconut milk and heat through, taking care not to let the soup boil. Serve hot or cold, garnished with cilantro and slices of lime.

i

preparation time
15 minutes

cooking time
30 minutes

**nutritional value
per serve**
fat: 5.1 g
carbohydrate: 4 g
protein: 1.5 g

curried cream of vegetable soup

ingredients

3 tablespoons peanut oil
2 tablespoons curry powder
pinch of ground cinnamon
pinch of nutmeg
pinch of turmeric
pinch of ginger
3 carrots, diced
2 onions, chopped
2 cloves garlic, chopped
2 potatoes, diced
2 small zucchini, diced
1 litre (1^2/$_3$ pints) vegetable stock
300 g (10 oz) can cannellini beans, drained
220 g (7^1/$_2$ oz) can red kidney beans, drained
185 ml (6 fl oz) crème fraîche
salt
2 teaspoons flat-leaf parsley, chopped for garnish
serves 4

i

preparation time
20 minutes

cooking time
30 minutes

nutritional value per serve
fat: 4.3 g
carbohydrate: 5.7 g
protein: 2.8 g

1 In a large heavy-bottomed saucepan, place the oil and add the curry powder, cinnamon, nutmeg, turmeric and ginger. Cook for 1 minute, then add carrots, onions, garlic, potatoes and zucchini. Stir to coat thoroughly in the oil and spice mixture, and cook for a further 5 minutes. Add the stock and bring to the boil. Reduce the heat and simmer for 20 minutes or until the vegetables are tender.

2 Add the cannellini and red kidney beans and gently heat through. Remove from the heat and stir in the crème fraîche. Season with salt and pepper to taste and serve sprinkled with the parsley.

thai hot and sour shrimp soup

ingredients

2 stalks lemon grass
300 g (10 oz) green shrimp, with head and shell on
1 tablespoon vegetable oil
1 litre (1²/₃ pints) chicken stock
1 clove garlic, minced
1 inch piece fresh root ginger, roughly chopped
grated zest of 1 lime and juice of 2 limes
1 green chilli pepper, deseeded and finely chopped
salt and black pepper
1 tablespoon thai fish sauce
1 red chilli pepper, deseeded and sliced
2 tablespoons chopped cilantro to garnish

serves 4

i

preparation time
25 minutes

cooking time
30 minutes

nutritional value per serve
fat: 1.6 g
carbohydrate: 0.6 g
protein: 5.1 g

1 Peel the outer layers from the lemon grass stalks and chop the lower white bulbous parts into 3 pieces, discarding the fibrous tops. Shell the shrimp, leaving the tails attached and reserving the shells for the stock. Cut a slit along the back of each shrimp with a sharp knife and remove the thin black vein. Rinse the shrimp, then refrigerate until needed.

2 In a large saucepan, heat the oil and fry the shrimp shells for 2–3 minutes, until pink. Add the stock, garlic, ginger, lemon grass, lime zest, green chilli pepper and salt to taste. Bring to the boil, then reduce the heat, cover and simmer for 20 minutes.

3 Strain the stock and return to the pan. Stir in fish sauce and lime juice and bring to the boil. Add the shrimp, reduce the heat and simmer for 3 minutes or until the shrimp turn pink and are cooked through. Season with pepper and serve garnished with red chilli pepper and cilantro.

vegetable saffron samosas

ingredients

vegetable saffron filling
1 tablespoon peanut oil
1 teaspoon sesame oil
1 onion, finely chopped
1 tablespoon finely grated fresh ginger
1 teaspoon ground cumin
1 potato, peeled and finely chopped
1 carrot, finely chopped
1/4 teaspoon saffron threads, soaked in
    1 tablespoon hot water
1 red bell pepper, finely chopped
60 g (2 oz) frozen peas

pastry
315 g (10 oz) flour
1 tablespoon baking powder
1 tablespoon superfine sugar
4 tablespoons lard
1 cup (250 ml, 8 fl oz) warm water

sun-dried bell pepper dipping sauce
125 g (4 oz) sun-dried bell peppers,
    chopped
1 cup (250 ml, 8 fl oz) mayonnaise
1 tablespoon white-wine vinegar

makes 20

1 To make filling, heat peanut and sesame oils together in a wok over medium heat, add onion, ginger and cumin and stir-fry for 3 minutes or until onion is golden. In a bowl, combine potato, carrot and saffron. Add to wok and stir-fry for 10 minutes until potato is tender Add red bell pepper and peas and stir-fry for another 5 minutes. Remove mixture from wok and set aside to cool.

2 To make pastry, place flour, baking powder, sugar and lard in a food processor and process until mixture resembles fine breadcrumbs. With machine running, gradually add water and process until mixture forms a soft dough. Turn dough onto a lightly floured surface and knead until smooth and glossy. Cover and rest for 10 minutes.

3 Divide dough into 20 equal pieces and shape into balls. Roll out each dough ball to form a 4 inch circle. Place a tablespoon of filling on one half leaving a 1/2 inch border. Brush edges lightly with water, fold pastry over filling and press edges together to seal.

4 Half fill a clean wok with hot water and bring to the boil. Place samosas in a bamboo steamer lined with nonstick baking paper. Pierce holes in the paper to allow steam through. Cover steamer, place on a wire rack in wok and steam for 10 minutes or until pastry is cooked.

5 To make sauce, place sun-dried bell peppers, mayonnaise and vinegar in a food processor or blender and process until smooth.

i

preparation time
20 minutes

cooking time
28 minutes

nutritional value
per serve
fat: 10.6 g
carbohydrate: 25 g
protein: 4.1 g

hot and sour fish soup

ingredients

1 kg (2 lb) firm fleshed fish (red snapper)
1¹/₂ tablespoons fish sauce
¹/₄ teaspoon white pepper
1 green onion, chopped
1.5 litres (2¹/₂ pints) water
2 stalks lemon grass, cut into 2 inch
   lengths and crushed lightly
55 g (2 oz) tamarind pulp
³/₄ cup (185 ml, 6 fl oz) boiling water
1 tablespoon sugar
185 g (6 oz) bamboo shoots, sliced
160 g (5¹/₂ oz) pineapple, sliced
2 tomatoes, cut into wedges
90 g (3 oz) beansprouts
2 handfuls mixed vietnamese herbs
   (cilantro, bitter herb, asian basil)
1 lime, cut into wedges to serve
1 chilli pepper, sliced to serve
serves 4-6

1 Remove head, fins and tail from fish and cut into 8–10 large pieces. In a bowl, combine fish, fish sauce, pepper and green onion. Set aside to marinate for 15 minutes.

2 Place 6 cups water in a large saucepan and bring to the boil. Add the fish with the marinade and lemon grass. Reduce heat and simmer for 20 minutes. In a bowl, combine tamarind pulp and the ³/₄ cup boiling water and allow to soak for 15 minutes.

3 Strain the tamarind pulp through a fine strainer, discarding the pulp. Add to the saucepan along with the sugar, bamboo shoots, pineapple and tomatoes. Simmer for 4–5 minutes until fish is tender.

4 Divide bean sprouts between serving bowls and spoon over hot soup. Sprinkle over mixed vietnamese herbs. Serve with lime wedges and sliced chilli pepper on the side.

i

preparation time
30 minutes,
plus 15 minutes
marinating
cooking time
15 minutes

**nutritional value
per serve**
fat: 0.7 g
carbohydrate: 2 g
protein: 6.1 g

warm thai lamb salad

ingredients

250 g (8 oz) assorted lettuce leaves, washed and crisped
1 cucumber, sliced lengthwise into thin ribbons
2 teaspoons vegetable oil
500 g (1 lb) lamb fillets, trimmed and thinly sliced

cilantro and chilli dressing
2 tablespoons chopped cilantro
1 tablespoon light brown sugar
4 tablespoons soy sauce
2 tablespoons sweet chilli sauce
2 tablespoons lime juice
2 teaspoons fish sauce

serves 4

1 In a bowl, combine cilantro, sugar, soy and chilli sauces, lime juice and fish sauce. Set aside.

2 Arrange lettuce leaves and cucumber on a serving platter and set aside.

3 Heat oil in a wok over a high heat, add lamb and stir-fry for 2 minutes or until brown. Place lamb on top of lettuce leaves, drizzle with dressing and serve immediately.

preparation time
10 minutes

cooking time
2 minutes

nutritional value per serve
fat: 2.7 g
carbohydrate: 2.6 g
protein: 10.6 g

poultry
and
meat

creamy chicken korma

ingredients

3 tablespoons vegetable oil
1 onion, chopped
2 cloves garlic, minced
3 tablespoons all purpose flour
2 tablespoons mild korma curry powder
750 g (1½ lb) chicken breast fillets,
    cut into 1 inch cubes
350 ml (11½ fl oz) chicken stock
25 g (1 oz) raisins
1 tablespoon chopped cilantro
1 teaspoon garam masala
juice of ½ lemon
4 tablespoons sour cream
fried onion rings for garnish (optional)
serves 4

preparation time
15 minutes
cooking time
30 minutes
**nutritional value
per serve**
fat: 7.8 g
carbohydrate: 4.1 g
protein: 12 g

1 Heat the oil in a large bottomed saucepan, add the onion and garlic and cook gently for 5 minutes or until softened.

2 Into a bowl, place the flour and curry powder and mix together. Toss the chicken in the seasoned flour, coating well. Reserve the remaining flour. Add the chicken to the onion and garlic, then cook, stirring, for 3–4 minutes until lightly browned. Stir in the seasoned flour and cook for 1 minute.

3 Add the stock and raisins and bring to the boil, stirring. Cover and simmer for 15 minutes. Add the cilantro and garam masala and cook for a further 5 minutes. Remove the pan from the heat and stir in the lemon juice and sour cream. Return to a low heat and warm through, taking care not to let the mixture boil.

fragrant duck with pineapple

ingredients

2 (about 175 g, 6 oz each) boneless duck
  breasts, skinned and cut into strips
1 teaspoon five-spice powder
2 tablespoons soy sauce
2 tablespoons rice wine or dry sherry
1 teaspoon sugar
1 tablespoon peanut oil
1 red bell pepper, deseeded and
  cut into thin strips
2 inch piece fresh ginger, cut into
  matchsticks
2 green onions, white and green parts
separated, thinly shredded
175 g (6 oz) fresh pineapple, cut into
  bite-sized pieces, plus juice
salt
serves 4

1 Place the duck, five-spice powder, soy sauce, rice wine or sherry and sugar in a shallow non-metallic dish. Cover and marinate for 20 minutes.

2 Remove the duck from the marinade and reserve the marinade. Heat oil in a wok. Stir-fry duck over a high heat for 2 minutes. Add bell pepper, ginger and white part of onions and stir-fry for a further 3–4 minutes until bell pepper starts to soften.

3 Add pineapple and juice to the wok. Add marinade and stir-fry for 1–2 minutes. Season with salt if necessary. Serve straight away, sprinkled with the green part of the onions. Serve with plain boiled noodles.

i

preparation time
20 minutes,
plus 20 minutes
marinating

cooking time
10 minutes

**nutritional value
per serve**
fat: 6.2 g
carbohydrate: 4.3 g
protein: 8.6 g

chicken stir-fry with lemon and mango

ingredients

1 ripe mango
2 tablespoons sunflower oil
2 cloves garlic, minced
1 inch piece fresh root ginger, finely chopped
4 chicken breast fillets, cut into strips
150 g (5 oz) sugar snap peas, halved lengthways
2 celery stalks, thinly sliced
1 yellow bell pepper, deseeded and cut into matchsticks
4 green onions, thinly sliced
sea salt and freshly ground black pepper
juice of 1/2 lemon
2 teaspoons white wine or apple juice
1 tablespoon balsamic vinegar
1 tablespoon clear honey
2 tablespoons chopped cilantro
serves 4

i

preparation time
25 minutes

cooking time
10 minutes

nutritional value
fat: 4.4 g
carbohydrate: 3.1 g
protein: 14.1 g

1 Slice the two fatter 'cheeks' of the mango from either side of the stone. Cut a criss-cross pattern across the flesh of each piece to divide into small cubes, then push the skin upwards and slice off the cubes. Set aside.

2 Heat the oil in a wok or large skillet until hot. Add garlic, ginger and chicken and stir fry for 3 minutes. Add sugar snap peas, celery and bell pepper and stir-fry for 3–4 minutes. Add the green onions, mangos and seasoning, and then stir-fry for a further 2 minutes.

3 In a small bowl, combine the lemon juice, white wine or apple juice, balsamic vinegar and honey. Add to the wok and continue to cook for a further 2 minutes. Add the cilantro and serve.

beef curry

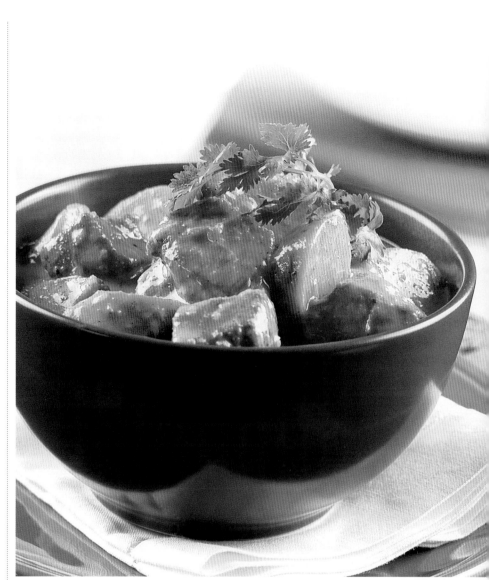

ingredients

1 kg (2 lb) stewing beef
1 large onion, sliced
4 cloves garlic, minced
2 tablespoons chopped ginger
2 red chilli peppers, seeded and
  chopped finely
$3^1/_2$ tablespoons hot curry powder
2 teaspoons turmeric
1 teaspoon black ground pepper
$1^1/_2$ teaspoons salt
$^1/_3$ cup (80 ml, $2^3/_4$ fl oz) vegetable oil
1 cup (250 ml, 8 fl oz) water
$4^1/_2$ tablespoons fish sauce
1 tablespoon sugar
3 large carrots, chopped
3 tablespoons cornstarch
$2^1/_4$ cups (560 ml, $18^1/_2$ fl oz) coconut
  milk
cilantro leaves to garnish
serves 4

i

preparation time
15 minutes,
plus 12 hours
marinating

cooking time
15 minutes

**nutritional value
per serve**
fat: 9.7 g
carbohydrate: 2.7 g
protein: 17.1 g

1 Cut the beef into cubes and place in a non-metallic container. Add onion, garlic, ginger, chilli peppers, curry powder, turmeric, pepper and 1 teaspoon of salt, mix and cover with plastic wrap to dry marinate for 12 hours or overnight. Turn occasionally.

2 In a large, heavy-bottomed saucepan, heat oil on high, add beef, turning to seal all sides. Add the water, $^1/_2$ teaspoon salt and fish sauce. Bring to the boil, turn heat to low, cover and simmer for 1 hour. Add sugar and carrots and continue cooking for 15–20 minutes until meat is tender.

3 Blend cornstarch with a little coconut milk, add to the rest of the coconut milk and pour into the curry. Stir for 10–15 minutes until thickened. Transfer to a serving dish and garnish with cilantro leaves.

beef with black bean sauce

ingredients

450 g (14 oz) sirloin or rump steak,
  cut into thin strips
1 clove garlic, minced
1 small red chilli pepper, deseeded and
  finely chopped (optional)
1 tablespoon dark soy sauce
black pepper
2 teaspoons cornstarch
1 tablespoon white-wine vinegar
2 tablespoons vegetable oil
1 red bell pepper, deseeded and
  cut into strips
1 yellow bell pepper, deseeded and cut
  into strips
1 small zucchini, cut into
  matchsticks
150 g (5 oz) sugar snap peas, sliced
3 tablespoons black bean stir-fry sauce
4 green onions, diagonally sliced
serves 4

i

preparation time
15 minutes

cooking time
15 minutes

nutritional value
per serve
fat: 5.1 g
carbohydrate: 3.5 g
protein: 9.4 g

1 In a bowl, combine steak strips, garlic, chilli (if using), soy sauce and seasoning. In another bowl, mix the cornstarch with 1 tablespoon of water until smooth, then stir in vinegar.

2 Heat the oil in a wok or large skillet until very hot. Add the meat and its marinade and stir-fry for 4 minutes, tossing continuously, until seared on all sides.

3 Add bell pepper and stir-fry for 2 minutes. Stir in zucchini and sugar snap peas and cook for 3 minutes. Reduce the heat and add the cornstarch mixture and black bean sauce. Stir to mix thoroughly and cook for 2 minutes or until the meat and vegetables are cooked through. Scatter with green onions just before serving. Serve over egg noodles if desired.

roasted tandoori chicken breasts

ingredients

1 teaspoon salt
2 cloves garlic, chopped
1 inch piece fresh root ginger, chopped
1 tablespoon chopped cilantro
1 tablespoon chopped fresh mint
1/2 teaspoon turmeric
1/2 teaspoon hot chilli powder
2 cardamom pods, split, husks
    discarded and seeds reserved
4 tablespoons natural yogurt
juice of 1/2 lemon
4 chicken fillets
extra cilantro leaves to garnish
serves 4

i

preparation time
15 minutes, plus
6 hours
marinating

cooking time
25 minutes

**nutritional value
per serve**
fat: 5.3 g
carbohydrate: 0.4 g
protein: 19.9 g

1 Grind the salt, garlic, ginger, cilantro, mint, turmeric, chilli powder and cardamom seeds to a paste, using a pestle and mortar or coffee grinder. Transfer to a large, non-metallic container, stir in the yogurt and lemon juice and mix together well.

2 Score each chicken breast 4 times with a sharp knife, then add to the marinade and turn to coat thoroughly. Cover and chill for 6 hours, or overnight.

3 Preheat the oven to 220°C (425°F, gas mark 7). Place the chicken breasts on a rack in a roasting pan and cook for 20–25 minutes, until tender and the juices run clear when pierced with a skewer. Serve with naan bread and salad.

green banana chicken curry

ingredients

salt
1 teaspoon ground turmeric
10 green bananas (plantain), peeled
2 tablespoons vegetable oil
3 green onions, chopped
1 tablespoon finely grated fresh ginger
2 small fresh red chilli peppers, seeded
   and chopped
1¹/₂ cups (375 ml, 12 fl oz) coconut milk
1 cinnamon stick
45 g (1¹/₂ oz) seedless golden raisins
30 g (1 oz) roasted cashews
6 chicken breast fillets, cut into thin
   strips

serves 6

1 Combine salt and turmeric and rub over bananas. Heat oil in a wok over a medium heat, add 5 bananas and stir-fry for 5 minutes or until brown. Remove bananas from pan and drain on absorbent kitchen paper. Repeat with remainder adding extra oil if needed.

2 Add green onions, ginger and chillies to pan and stir-fry for 2 minutes or until mixture is soft. Stir in coconut milk, cinnamon, raisins, cashews and chicken. Simmer, stirring occasionally, for 20 minutes.

3 Slice bananas, return to pan and simmer, stirring occasionally, for 10 minutes or until chicken is tender. Remove cinnamon stick before serving.

i

preparation time
10 minutes

cooking time
30 minutes

**nutritional value
per serve**
fat: 6.7 g
carbohydrate: 7 g
protein: 13 g

thai green duck curry with bamboo shoots

ingredients

2 tablespoons vegetable oil
3 tablespoons thai green curry paste
4 boneless duck breasts, skinned and
   cut into 1 inch cubes
400 ml (13 fl oz) can coconut milk
225 g (7½ oz) can sliced bamboo shoots,
   drained
2 tablespoons thai fish sauce
1 teaspoon light brown sugar
salt
2 tablespoons chopped fresh basil
4 tablespoons chopped cilantro
extra basil leaves to garnish

serves 4

1 Heat the oil in a large, heavy-bottomed saucepan. Add curry paste and fry, stirring frequently, for 3 minutes or until the aromas are released. Add duck, turn to coat thoroughly, and fry for 4–5 minutes, stirring from time to time.

2 Stir in coconut milk, bamboo shoots, fish sauce, sugar and salt to taste. Bring to the boil, stirring often, then reduce the heat. Simmer, uncovered, for 30–35 minutes until the duck is tender, stirring occasionally. Just before serving, stir in the chopped basil and cilantro, and garnish with basil leaves.

i

preparation time
10 minutes

cooking time
45 minutes

**nutritional value
per serve**
fat: 18.3 g
carbohydrate: 2 g
protein: 10.4 g

glazed pork spare ribs

ingredients

1 tablespoon soy sauce

2 tablespoons white-wine vinegar

3 tablespoons hoi sin or oyster sauce

2 tablespoons honey

2 cloves garlic, minced

1 inch piece fresh ginger root, peeled and grated

2 teaspoons vegetable oil

1/2 teaspoon five-spice powder

1 tablespoon light brown sugar

1.5 -2 kg (3-4 lb) american style pork spareribs

serves 6

1 In a saucepan, combine soy sauce, white-wine vinegar, hoi sin or oyster sauce, honey, garlic, ginger, oil, five-spice powder and sugar. Stir well and bring to the boil. Remove from heat. Place pork in a large pie dish. Spread half of the marinade over the ribs to cover all surfaces. Cover and stand 30 minutes.

2 Preheat the oven to 220°C (425°F, gas mark 7). Place the ribs on a rack in a baking pan and pour some water under the rack to prevent drippings from charring. Bake for 30 minutes. Reduce heat to 180°C (350°F, gas mark 4) and bake for 40 minutes, brushing well with remaining marinade every 15 minutes to glaze. Serve immediately.

i

preparation time
10 minutes, plus 30 minutes marinating

cooking time
1 hour 10 minutes

nutritional value per serve
fat: 15.8 g
carbohydrate: 3.4 g
protein: 24.5 g

fried noodles with chicken stir-fry

ingredients

200 g (7 oz) wheat noodles
250 g (8 oz) chicken breast fillets
    cut into 2 inch wide strips
½ teaspoon salt
½ teaspoon five-spice powder
2 tablespoons oil
1 clove garlic, halved
1 red bell pepper, deseeded
    and cut into strips
4 mushrooms, sliced
4 green onions
2 baby bok choy (pak choi), leaves
    separated
425 g (14 oz) can baby corn, drained
1 tablespoon dry sherry
2 teaspoons cornstarch
1 tablespoon oyster sauce

serves 4

i

preparation time
15 minutes

cooking time
6 minutes

**nutritional value
per serve**
fat: 3.9 g
carbohydrate: 15 g
protein: 6.5 g

1 Soak wheat noodles in hot water for 5 minutes, drain well. Sprinkle chicken strips with salt and five-spice powder.

2 Heat the wok, add 2 teaspoons of oil. Place in the noodles and stir-fry until hot and colored a little. Remove and keep hot.

3 Add 2 teaspoons of oil to the wok, add garlic and fry for 1 minute then remove. Add chicken and stir-fry for 2 minutes. Remove and keep hot.

4 Add more oil to the wok if needed. Add bell peppers, mushrooms and green onions, and stir-fry for 1 minute. Toss in bok choy and baby corn.

5 In a small bowl, combine sherry and cornstarch until smooth, add oyster sauce. Return chicken to the wok and toss, stir in blended sauce and toss well to distribute. Stir-fry for 1–2 minutes to thicken and reheat. Pile over hot noodles and serve immediately.

chicken laksa

ingredients

$^1/_3$ cup (90 ml, 3 fl oz) vegetable oil

4 small fresh red chilli peppers, finely
chopped

1 stalk fresh lemon grass, finely
chopped or $^1/_2$ teaspoon dried lemon
grass, soaked in hot water until soft

3 cloves garlic, minced

2 tablespoons finely grated fresh ginger

1 teaspoon ground cumin

1 teaspoon ground turmeric

6 candlenuts or unsalted macadamia nuts

$^1/_4$ teaspoon shrimp paste

1 litre ($1^2/_3$ pints) coconut milk

4 boneless chicken breast fillets, cut
into 1 inch cubes

2 tablespoons chopped cilantro

375 g (12 oz) rice noodles, cooked

125 g (4 oz) bean sprouts

125 g (4 oz) fried tofu, sliced

serves 4

i

preparation time
20 minutes

cooking time
15 minutes

**nutritional value
per serve**
fat: 14.9 g
carbohydrate: 4 g
protein: 10.5 g

1 Into a food processor place 2 tablespoons oil, chilli peppers, lemon grass, garlic, ginger, cumin, turmeric, candlenuts or macadamia nuts and shrimp paste and process to make a smooth paste.

2 In a large saucepan, heat the remaining oil over a medium heat, add paste and cook, stirring, for 2 minutes or until fragrant. Stir in coconut milk and simmer, stirring occasionally, for 15 minutes or until mixture thickens slightly.

3 Add chicken and cilantro and simmer, stirring occasionally, for 15 minutes longer or until chicken is tender. To serve, divide rice noodles between serving bowls, top with bean sprouts and tofu, pour over coconut milk mixture and serve immediately.

seafood

chinese-style steamed grey mullet

ingredients

1 grey mullet, about 700 g (1 lb 7 oz),
  scaled and gutted
½ teaspoon salt
1 tablespoon vegetable oil
1 tablespoon light soy sauce
1 large carrot, cut into fine strips
4 green onions, cut into fine strips
1 tablespoon grated fresh root ginger
1 tablespoon sesame oil (optional)
cilantro to garnish

serves 2

1 In a small bowl, combine salt, vegetable oil and soy sauce. Make 4 deep slashes along each side of the fish, and rub inside and out with the sauce mixture. Cover and place in the refrigerator for 30 minutes.

i

preparation time
10 minutes,
plus 30 minutes
refrigeration

cooking time
20 minutes

**nutritional value
per serve**
fat: 8.8 g
carbohydrate: 0.8 g
protein: 15.4 g

2 Spread half the carrot, green onions and ginger in the center of a large piece of foil. Place the fish on top, then sprinkle with the remaining vegetables and ginger and any remaining oil mixture.

3 Loosely fold over the foil and seal. Transfer the fish to a steamer or a rack set over a roasting pan half filled with water. Cover the steamer tightly with a lid or the roasting pan with foil. Cook for 20 minutes or until the fish is firm and cooked through. Put the sesame oil, if using, into a small saucepan and heat. Drizzle over the fish and garnish with cilantro.

shrimp, sugar snap pea and mango stir-fry

ingredients

400 g (13 oz) green shrimp, peeled
2 tablespoons vegetable oil
1½ tablespoons finely grated fresh root
    ginger
300 g (10 oz) sugar snap peas
    (mangetout)
bunch of green onions, sliced
1 large ripe mango, peeled and thinly
    sliced
2 tablespoons light soy sauce
serves 4

1 Cut a slit along the back of each shrimp with a sharp knife and remove any thin black vein.

2 Heat the wok on a high heat, add oil, ginger and shrimp and stir-fry for 2 minutes or until the shrimp are just turning pink. Add the sugar snap peas and green onions and stir-fry for a further minute to soften slightly. Stir in the mango and soy sauce and stir-fry for 1 minute to heat through. Serve with steamed rice.

i

preparation time
15 minutes

cooking time
5 minutes

**nutritional value
per serve**
fat: 3.6 g
carbohydrate: 4.2 g
protein: 8.6 g

1 In a bowl, combine lime juice, rice wine and garlic. Add scallops and set aside for 15 minutes. In a wok, heat the sesame oil. Add ginger, green onions, mushrooms and bell pepper. Stir-fry for about 3 minutes until ginger is fragrant.

2 Add scallops and marinade, and stir-fry for 3 minutes until scallops have become opaque. Add soy sauce and pepper to taste. In a cup, combine cornstarch and water to a paste. Add paste to wok and cook while stirring until sauce thickens slightly. Serve immediately with steamed white rice.

ginger scallop stir-fry

ingredients

2 tablespoons fresh lime juice
2 tablespoons rice wine
1 clove garlic, minced
250 g (8 oz) fresh scallops
1 tablespoon sesame oil
2 teaspoons finely grated
    fresh root ginger
4 green onions, cut diagonally into $1/2$
inch lengths
90 g (3 oz) button mushrooms, sliced
$1/2$ red bell pepper, diced
2 teaspoons soy sauce
pepper
1 teaspoon cornstarch
2 tablespoons water
serves 4

i

preparation time
20 minutes

cooking time
8 minutes

**nutritional value
per serve**
fat: 3.7 g
carbohydrate: 2 g
protein: 6.4 g

southeast asian pan-fried shrimp

ingredients

500 g (1 lb) green shrimp
3 small red chilli peppers, deseeded and
  chopped
2 cloves garlic, chopped
1 inch piece fresh root ginger, chopped
1 green onion, chopped
2 tablespoons peanut oil
1 onion, chopped
2 tomatoes, quartered
1 teaspoon sugar
salt
serves 4

i

preparation time
25 minutes

cooking time
8 minutes

**nutritional value
per serve**
fat: 4.1 g
carbohydrate: 1.9 g
protein: 10.2 g

1 Shell the shrimp, leaving the tails attached. Cut a slit along the back of each shrimp with a sharp knife and remove the thin black vein. Rinse well and refrigerate. In a food processor, blend the chilli peppers, garlic, ginger and green onion to a paste.

2 Heat a wok over a high heat, add oil and onion and fry for 2 minutes to soften slightly. Add paste and stir-fry for 1 minute to release the flavors. Add shrimp and tomatoes, mixing thoroughly, then sprinkle over sugar and salt to taste. Stir-fry for 3–5 minutes, until shrimp turn pink and are cooked through.

thai fish cakes with peanut dipping sauce

ingredients

350 g (11½ oz) skinless cod fillets
1 tablespoon thai red curry paste
1 tablespoon thai fish sauce
2 tablespoons cornstarch
1 medium egg, beaten
1 green onion, finely chopped
60 g (2 oz) fine green beans, cut into ⅛ inch lengths
peanut oil for shallow-frying

dipping sauce
2 tablespoons sugar
juice of 1 lime
1 clove garlic, finely chopped
⅓ inch piece fresh root ginger, finely chopped
1 tablespoon roughly crushed roasted salted peanuts
1 small red chilli pepper, deseeded and finely chopped
2 tablespoons light soy sauce

serves 4

i

preparation time
20 minutes

cooking time
16 minutes

nutritional value per serve
fat: 16.9 g
carbohydrate: 7.5 g
protein: 9.8 g

1 In a food processor, finely mince the cod fillets. Add red curry paste, fish sauce, cornstarch and egg. Blend briefly or stir until mixed. Transfer to a bowl and combine with green onions and beans.

2 Lightly oil your hands (it's quite sticky), then divide mixture and shape into 8 patties. In a bowl, combine sugar and lime juice, stirring until sugar dissolves. Stir in garlic, ginger, peanuts, chilli pepper and soy sauce. Set aside.

3 Heat ¼ inch of oil in a large skillet over a medium to high heat, then fry half of the fish cakes for 3–4 minutes on each side, until golden. Drain on kitchen paper, then cook remaining cakes. Serve with dipping sauce.

baked cod with ginger and green onions

ingredients

oil for greasing
500 g (1 lb) piece cod fillet
1 tablespoon light soy sauce
1 tablespoon rice wine or medium-dry
  sherry
1 teaspoon sesame oil
salt
3 green onions, shredded and cut into 1
inch pieces, white and green parts
  separated
1 inch piece fresh root ginger,
  finely chopped
serves 4

1 Preheat the oven to 190°C (375°F, gas mark 5). Line a shallow baking pan with a piece of lightly greased foil to come past the sides of the baking pan. Place the cod on the pan, skin-side down. Pour over the soy sauce, rice wine or sherry, oil and salt to taste, then sprinkle over white part of green onion and ginger.

2 Loosely wrap the foil over the fish, folding the edges together to seal. Bake for 20–25 minutes, until cooked through and tender. Unwrap the parcel, transfer the fish to a serving plate and sprinkle over remaining green onions.

preparation time
10 minutes

cooking time
25 minutes

**nutritional value
per serve**
fat: 1.4 g
carbohydrate: 0.6 g
protein: 15.1 g

seafood with oyster mushrooms

ingredients

125 g (4 oz) small calamari (squid) hoods
8 baby octopus
8 medium-sized green shrimp, shelled and deveined
155 g (5 oz) fresh scallops
2 teaspoons vegetable oil
250 g (8 oz) oyster mushrooms
6 green onions, chopped
freshly ground black pepper

marinade

3 tablespoons chopped cilantro
2 cloves garlic, minced
4 tablespoons worcestershire sauce
⅓ cup (90 ml, 3 fl oz) soy sauce
2 tablespoons sweet chilli sauce

serves 4-6

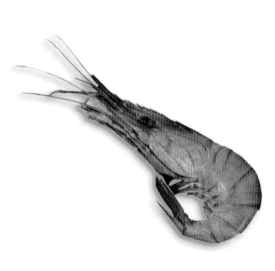

preparation time
15 minutes, plus
2-3 hours
marinating

cooking time
5 minutes

nutritional value per serve
fat: 1.5 g
carbohydrate: 3.2 g
protein: 10.7 g

1 Cut down the length of the squid's hood and open out. Score the inside surface into a diamond pattern taking care not to cut right through to the flesh. Clean the baby octopus by cutting off the head below the eyes and discard. Push out and remove the beak located in the center of the tentacles. Wash well.

2 In a bowl, combine all marinade ingredients and add squid, octopus, shrimp and scallops. Toss to coat with marinade, cover and refrigerate for 2–3 hours.

3 Drain seafood and reserve the marinade. Heat a wok until very hot, add oil swirling to coat base and sides. Add squid and octopus and stir-fry for 2 minutes then add shrimp and scallops. Stir-fry for 1 minute.

4 Add mushrooms, green onions and 3 tablespoons reserved marinade and stir-fry for 2 minutes more. Season to taste with black pepper. Transfer to a serving dish and serve immediately.

lime fish with noodles

ingredients

2 teaspoons vegetable oil

3 green onions, chopped

1 stalk fresh lemon grass, chopped or
$\frac{1}{2}$ teaspoon dried lemon grass,
soaked in hot water until soft

1 fresh red chilli pepper, chopped

750 g ($1\frac{1}{2}$ lb) firm white fish fillets, cut
into thick strips

2 tablespoons lime juice

315 g (10 oz) fresh rice noodles

$\frac{1}{2}$ bunch (250 g, 8 oz) bok choy
(pak choi), chopped

4 tablespoons water

2 tablespoons soy sauce

2 teaspoons white miso

serves 4

i

preparation time
10 minutes

cooking time
5 minutes

**nutritional value
per serve**
fat: 1.9 g
carbohydrate: 5.2 g
protein: 11.3 g

1 Heat wok over a high heat, add the oil, green onions, lemon grass and chilli pepper and stir-fry for 1 minute. Add fish and lime juice and stir-fry for 2 minutes or until fish is almost cooked. Remove fish mixture from wok and set aside.

2 Add noodles, bok choy, water, soy sauce and miso to wok and stir-fry for 2 minutes. Return fish mixture to wok and stir-fry for 1 minute or until heated through

oriental-style salmon fillets

ingredients

4 skinless salmon fillets
2 tablespoons vegetable oil
2 tablespoons light soy sauce
2 tablespoons clear honey
25 g (1 oz) stem ginger, drained and
 finely chopped
2 green onions, cut into long strips
finely grated zest and juice
 of $\frac{1}{2}$ lime
black pepper
lime wedges to serve
serves 4

preparation time
5 minutes,
plus 30 minutes
marinating

cooking time
8 minutes

**nutritional value
per serve**
fat: 11 g
carbohydrate: 8.5 g
protein: 13.7 g

1 Place the salmon fillets in a shallow non-metallic pan. Mix together the oil, soy sauce, honey, ginger, green onions, lime zest and juice and seasoning. Pour over the fillets and turn to coat. Cover and marinate in the refrigerator for 30 minutes to 1 hour.

2 Preheat the broiler to high. Lightly oil a baking pan. Lift the fillets and green onions out of the marinade and place on the baking pan. Brush the fillets with a little of the marinade, then cook for 3 minutes. Turn over, brush with more of the marinade and broil for 3–5 minutes until cooked through. Garnish with lime wedges.

fragrant salmon stir-fry

ingredients

250 g (8 oz) skinless salmon fillets
1¹/₂ tablespoons peanut or sunflower oil
1 tablespoon chilled butter, cubed
marinade
1 stalk lemon grass
1 tablespoon soy sauce
¹/₂ cup (125 ml, 4 fl oz) orange juice
1 tablespoon chopped fresh dill
1 tablespoon chopped fresh basil
1 teaspoon grated fresh root ginger
1 clove garlic, minced
salt and black pepper
serves 2

i

preparation time
10 minutes,
2 hours marinating

cooking time
10 minutes

nutritional value
per serve
fat: 12.6 g
carbohydrate: 2.5 g
protein: 11.2 g

1 Peel the outer layer from the lemon grass stalk, then finely chop the lower white bulbous part. In a bowl, combine lemon grass, soy sauce, orange juice, ¹/₂

tablespoon dill, ¹/₂ tablespoon basil, ginger, garlic and seasoning. Cut the salmon fillet into strips 1 inch wide and 3 inches long. Arrange strips in a shallow non-metallic pan and pour over marinade, turning strips to coat. Cover and refrigerate for 2 hours.

2 Remove salmon from pan and set aside the marinade. Pat salmon dry. Heat the oil in a large, heavy-bottomed skillet over a medium to high heat, add salmon and cook for 2 minutes on each side.

3 Arrange salmon on serving plates. Pour reserved marinade into the skillet, bring to the boil and simmer for 2 minutes. Beat in butter, a cube at a time. Spoon sauce over the salmon and sprinkle over remaining dill and basil.

singapore noodles with shrimp and ham

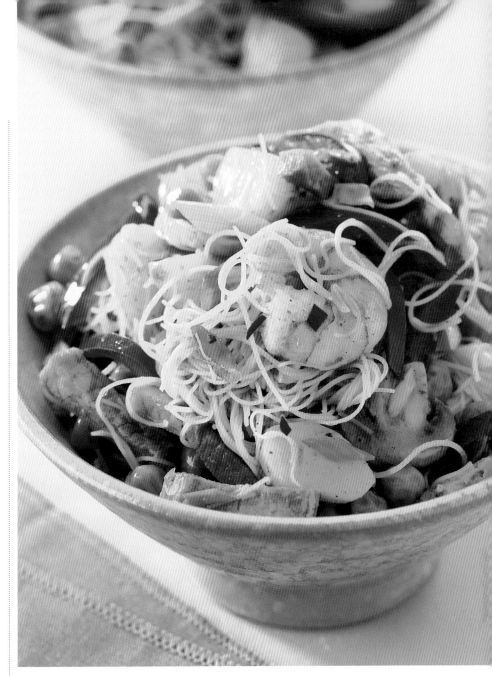

ingredients

250 g (8 oz) fresh stir-fry rice noodles
3 tablespoons vegetable oil
1 red chilli pepper, deseeded and finely chopped
4 tablespoons singapore fried noodle paste
2 tablespoons white-wine vinegar
1 tablespoon sugar
1 red bell pepper, deseeded and thinly sliced
175 g (6 oz) button mushrooms, sliced
225 g (7½ oz) cooked ham, cut into strips
100 g (3½ oz) frozen peas
225 g (7½ oz) can water chestnuts, drained and halved
225 g (8 oz) green shrimp, peeled
4 green onions, finely sliced

serves 4

---

i

preparation time
35 minutes

cooking time
10 minutes

nutritional value per serve
fat: 4.9 g
carbohydrate: 7.4 g
protein: 7.4 g

---

1 Prepare the noodles. Heat the wok or heavy-bottomed skillet until very hot. Add oil, chilli pepper, fried noodle paste, vinegar and sugar and cook for 1–2 minutes, stirring constantly to release the flavors. Add bell pepper and mushrooms and stir-fry for 3 minutes or until vegetables have softened.

2 Add ham, peas, water chestnuts and shrimp and stir-fry for 2–3 minutes until the shrimp turn pink. Add green onions and noodles. Cook for 1 minute, stirring, or until shrimp are cooked through and everything is hot.

vegetarian

curried vegetables

ingredients

2¹/₂ tablespoons vegetable oil
2 green onions, sliced thinly
3 cloves garlic, minced
3 tablespoons curry powder
2 teaspoons shrimp paste (optional)
2 stalks lemon grass, trimmed and thinly sliced
2 dried red chilli peppers, chopped
1 cup (250 ml, 8 fl oz) stock
1 cup (250 ml, 8 fl oz) coconut milk
1 tablespoon fish sauce
2 lime leaves or strips of lime or lemon peel
115 g (4 oz) carrots, cut diagonally into 1¹/₂ inch pieces
255 g (8 oz) potatoes, peeled and quartered
115 g (4 oz) green beans, topped and tailed
1 eggplant, cut into ¹/₂ inch cubes
salt
serves 4

i

preparation time
15 minutes
cooking time
15 minutes
nutritional value per serve
fat: 7.4 g
carbohydrate: 5.1 g
protein: 1.9 g

1 Heat oil in a heavy-bottomed pan, add green onions and garlic to saute until just golden. Add curry powder, shrimp paste if desired, lemon grass and chilli peppers and cook about 6 minutes. Add stock, coconut milk, fish sauce and lime leaves or citrus peel. Cover and bring to boil.

2 Reduce heat to medium, add carrots, potatoes, beans and eggplant, part-cover and simmer about 15 minutes until vegetables are tender and liquid has reduced.

spring vegetables in spiced coconut curry

ingredients

1 stalk lemon grass, peeled and white
   part finely chopped
2 tablespoons vegetable oil
$^1/_3$ inch piece fresh root ginger, chopped
1 onion, finely chopped
1 clove garlic, finely chopped
1 teaspoon turmeric
225 g ($7^1/_2$ oz) potatoes,
   cut into $^1/_2$ inch chunks
2 carrots, thickly sliced
400 ml (13 fl oz) can coconut milk
2 bay leaves
1 red chilli pepper, deseeded and finely
   chopped
salt
125 g (4 oz) baby sweetcorn, cobs,
   fresh or frozen
170 g ($5^1/_2$ oz) fine green beans
2 small zucchini, thickly sliced
2 tablespoons chopped cilantro

serves 4

1 Heat the oil in a large, heavy-bottomed saucepan. Add lemon grass, ginger, onion and garlic and fry for 5 minutes or until the onion and garlic have softened. Stir in turmeric, potatoes and carrots, then add the coconut milk, bay leaves, chilli pepper and salt. Bring to the boil, reduce the heat and simmer, partly covered, for 10 minutes, stirring occasionally.

2 Add sweetcorn and beans and simmer, partly covered, for 10 minutes. Add the zucchini and cook for a further 10 minutes or until all the vegetables are tender. Remove the bay leaves and garnish with cilantro just before serving.

preparation time
20 minutes

cooking time
35 minutes

nutritional value per serve
fat: 8.8 g
carbohydrate: 6.1 g
protein: 1.9 g

green vegetable stir-fry with sesame seeds

ingredients

2 tablespoons sesame seeds
2 tablespoons peanut oil
1 clove garlic, roughly chopped
1 inch piece fresh root ginger, finely chopped
150 g (5 oz) broccoli, cut into very small florets, peel and slice the thick stems
2 small zucchini, halved lengthways and finely sliced
170 g (5½ oz) sugar snap peas
1 tablespoon rice wine or medium-dry sherry
1 tablespoon dark soy sauce
1 tablespoon oyster sauce

serves 4

preparation time
10 minutes

cooking time
15 minutes

nutritional value per serve
fat: 7.8 g
carbohydrate: 2.9 g
protein: 3.3 g

1 Heat a wok, add sesame seeds and dry-fry for 2 minutes until golden, shaking the wok frequently. Remove and set aside. Add oil to the hot wok, then add garlic and ginger and stir-fry over a medium heat for 1–2 minutes until softened. Add broccoli and stir-fry for a further 2–3 minutes.

2 Add the zucchini and sugar snap peas and stir-fry for 3 minutes. Pour over the rice wine or sherry and sizzle for a minute. Add the soy and oyster sauces, mix well and stir-fry for 2 minutes. Sprinkle over toasted sesame seeds just before serving.

split lentil dhal with ginger and cilantro

ingredients

200 g (7 oz) dried split red lentils
$1/2$ teaspoon turmeric
1 tablespoon vegetable oil
$1/3$ inch piece fresh root ginger, finely chopped
1 teaspoon cumin seeds
1 teaspoon ground cilantro
salt and black pepper
4 tablespoons chopped cilantro
$1/2$ teaspoon paprika
extra cilantro to garnish
serves 4

1 Rinse the lentils and drain well, then place in a large saucepan with 850 ml ($1^1/2$ pints) of water. Bring to the boil, skimming off any scum, then stir in turmeric. Reduce the heat and partly cover the pan. Simmer for 30–35 minutes, until thickened, stirring occasionally.

2 Heat the oil in a small skillet. Add ginger and cumin seeds and fry for 30 seconds or until cumin seeds start to pop. Stir in ground coriander and fry for 1 minute.

3 Season the lentils with salt and pepper, then add the toasted spices. Stir in the chopped cilantro, mixing well. Transfer to a serving dish and garnish with the paprika and cilantro leaves.

preparation time
10 minutes

cooking time
40 minutes

nutritional value per serve
fat: 9.7 g
carbohydrate: 32 g
protein: 20.9 g

herbed rice noodles with asparagus and peanuts

ingredients

3 tablespoons rice vinegar
1 tablespoon sugar
1 small spanish onion, finely sliced into rings
255 g (8 oz) dried rice noodles
2 bunches of asparagus
a handful fresh mint, chopped
a handful cilantro, chopped
1 continental cucumber, peeled, seeded and thinly sliced
6 green onions, finely sliced
3 roma tomatoes, finely diced
120 g (4 oz) roasted peanuts, lightly crushed
juice of 2 limes
2 teaspoons fish sauce
2 teaspoons olive oil
$1/2$ teaspoon chilli flakes

serves 4

_i_

preparation time
20 minutes, plus
1 hour marination

cooking tme
4 minutes

**nutritional value
per serve**
fat: 3.8 g
carbohydrate: 6 g
protein: 3 g

1 Whisk the rice vinegar and sugar together and pour over the onion rings. Allow to marinate for 1 hour, tossing frequently. Cook rice noodles in boiling water for 1–2 minutes then drain immediately and rinse under cold water. Cut into a manageable length with kitchen scissors.

2 Peel the tough skin off the lower third of the asparagus stalk with a potato peeler, then cut into $1/2$ inch lengths. Simmer asparagus in salted water for 2 minutes until bright green and crisp-tender. Rinse in cold water to refresh.

3 Toss the noodles with the onion and vinegar mixture while still warm. Add asparagus, mint, cilantro, cucumber, green onions, tomatoes and roasted peanuts and toss thoroughly. In a small bowl, beat the lime juice, fish sauce, oil and chilli flakes together and drizzle over the noodle salad. Serve at room temperature.

vegetable stir-fry with noodles

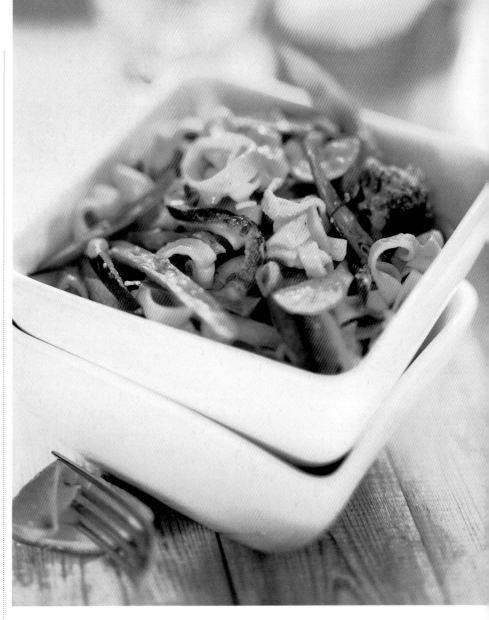

ingredients

250 g (8 oz) broad ribbon egg noodles
2 tablespoons sunflower oil
1 clove garlic, sliced
2 carrots, thinly sliced diagonally
150 g (5 oz) green beans, halved
150 g (5 oz) broccoli florets
1 red bell pepper, deseeded and
   cut into thin strips
4 green onions, thinly sliced diagonally

sauce

4 tablespoons smooth peanut butter
1 tablespoon tomato purée
1 tablespoon balsamic vinegar
sea salt and freshly ground black pepper
cilantro, chopped
lemon wedges, to serve

serves 4

1 Cook the noodles. In a bowl, combine the peanut butter, tomato purée, balsamic vinegar and seasoning with about 4 tablespoons of cold water. Set aside.

2 Heat a wok or large skillet until very hot. Add oil, garlic, carrots and green beans and stir-fry for 2 minutes, until lightly colored. Add broccoli and stir-fry for 2–3 minutes or until softened. Add bell pepper and green onions, then cook for a further 1 minute.

3 Add the sauce, 1/2 cup (125 ml, 4 fl oz) water and noodles. Combine well and stir-fry for 4–5 minutes or until everything is hot. Garnish with cilantro and serve with lemon wedges.

preparation time
25 minutes

cooking time
15 minutes

nutritional value per serve
fat: 9.1 g
carbohydrate: 15 g
protein: 6.5 g

root vegetable curry

ingredients

1 tablespoon olive oil
1 onion, chopped
1 green chilli pepper, deseeded and finely chopped
1 clove garlic, finely chopped
1 inch piece fresh root ginger, finely chopped
2 tablespoons plain flour
2 teaspoons ground coriander
2 teaspoons ground cumin
2 teaspoons turmeric
300 ml (10 fl oz) vegetable stock
200 ml (7 fl oz) can tomato puree
750 g (1½ lb) mixed root vegetables (potato, sweet potato, celeriac, swede etc), cubed
2 carrots, thinly sliced
black pepper
cilantro, chopped to garnish

serves 4

i

preparation time
20 minutes

cooking time
55 minutes

nutritional value per serve
fat: 1.4 g
carbohydrate: 9 g
protein: 1.8 g

1 Heat the oil in a large saucepan. Add the onion, chilli pepper, garlic and ginger and cook for 5 minutes or until softened, stirring occasionally. Stir in flour, coriander, cumin and turmeric and cook gently, stirring, for 1 minute to release the flavors.

2 Gradually stir in stock, then add tomato puree, root vegetables and carrots, season with black pepper and mix well. Bring to the boil, stirring, then cover, reduce heat and simmer for 45 minutes or until the vegetables are tender, stirring occasionally. Garnish with cilantro.

tofu and bok choy

ingredients

315 g (10 oz) firm tofu, cut into ½ inch
   cubes
60 g (2 oz) walnuts, roughly chopped
1 tablespoon finely grated fresh ginger
1 tablespoon chopped cilantro
4 tablespoons japanese soy sauce
1 teaspoon sesame oil
2 tablespoons vegetable oil
1 bunch (about 500 g, 1 lb) bok choy
   (pak choi), chopped
1 bunch (500 g, 1 lb) chinese broccoli,
   chopped
1 tablespoon oyster sauce
1 tablespoon sweet chilli sauce
serves 4

preparation time
10 minutes,
plus 2 hours
marination

cooking time
10 minutes

**nutritional value
per serve**
fat: 6.9 g
carbohydrate: 1.6 g
protein: 5.2 g

1 In a bowl, combine tofu, walnuts, ginger, cilantro, soy sauce and sesame oil. Cover and marinate at room temperature for 2 hours. Drain tofu and walnuts and reserve marinade.

2 Heat 1 tablespoon vegetable oil in a wok over a medium heat. Add bok choy and broccoli and stir-fry for 3 minutes or until just tender. Remove to a serving platter and keep warm.

3 Heat remaining oil in wok, add tofu and walnuts and stir-fry for 5 minutes or until tofu is golden. Add reserved marinade and oyster and chilli sauces, then stir-fry for 2 minutes. Place on top of vegetables. Serve immediately.

desserts

mango cake with nutmeg cream

ingredients

160 g (5½ oz) unsalted, roasted macadamia nuts
3 large mangoes
255 g (8 oz) butter
250 g (8 oz) superfine sugar
1 teaspoon vanilla essence
4 large eggs
250 g (8 oz) all purpose flour
1½ teaspoons baking powder
80 g (3 oz) roasted macadamia nuts, chopped
confectioners' sugar
2 cups (500 ml, 16 fl oz) pure cream
1 teaspoon nutmeg
1 mango, sliced, for serving

serves 6

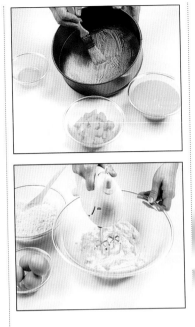

1 Preheat the oven to 180°C (350°F, gas mark 4) and butter a 8½ inch non-stick cake pan.

2 Crush 160 g (5⅓ oz) roasted macadamia nuts in a food processor and set aside. Peel the mangoes and dice the flesh, saving as much juice as possible. Reserve about ½ cup mango dices and purée the remainder (about 1 cup of mango purée).

3 Cream the softened butter and vanilla essence with ½ cup (125 g, 4 oz) sugar and beat until thick and pale. Add remaining sugar and beat until all sugar has been added. Add the eggs, one at a time, and beat well after each addition.

4 In a separate bowl, mix the crushed nuts, flour and baking powder together. Fold in the flour mixture, stirring well to combine. Add the mango purée and mix gently.

5 Spoon the batter into the pan. Sprinkle over chopped macadamia nuts and reserved diced mango and swirl through. Bake at 170°C (325°F) for 1 hour, remove from the oven and cool in the pan. When cool, remove cake from the pan. Dredge with confectioners' sugar. In a bowl, beat the cream and nutmeg together until the cream is thick and fragrant. Serve alongside the cake with some mango slices.

preparation time
15 minutes

cooking time
1 hour

nutritional value per serve
fat: 26.5 g
carbohydrate: 22 g
protein: 4 g

rum and lime banana fritters

ingredients

4 bananas
juice of 1 lime
2 teaspoons superfine sugar
1 tablespoon dark rum
oil for deep-frying
batter
100 g (3½ oz) cake flour
pinch of salt
150 ml (5 fl oz) water
2 tablespoons sesame seeds
serves 4

1 Peel each banana and cut in half crossways, then slice lengthways to make quarters. Place the banana quarters, lime juice, sugar and rum in a deep, non-metallic pan and mix gently. Cover and set aside for 30 minutes to marinate.

2 Sift the flour and salt into a mixing bowl. Pour in 150 ml (5 fl oz) water and beat to form a smooth, thick batter. Stir in the sesame seeds and set aside.

3 Heat 2 inches of oil in a wok or large skillet until smoking hot. Coat the banana pieces thoroughly in the batter. Fry for 5 minutes or until golden brown. Turn over and cook for 2 minutes to brown the other side. Drain on kitchen towels.

preparation time
10 minutes, plus 30 minutes marination

cooking time
15 minutes

nutritional value per serve
fat: 29.3 g
carbohydrate: 19 g
protein: 2.6 g

baked passion fruit custards

ingredients

4 large eggs, beaten
4 tablespoons superfine sugar
150 ml (5 fl oz) coconut milk
pinch of salt
2 passion fruit
serves 4

i

preparation time
10 minutes

cooking time
40 minutes

nutritional value per serve
fat: 11.1 g
carbohydrate: 15 g
protein: 6.9 g

1 Preheat the oven to 180°C (350°F, gas mark 4). Beat together the eggs, sugar, coconut milk and salt until smooth, then pour into 4 ramekins.

2 Halve 1 passion fruit, scoop out the pulp and seeds and divide between the 4 custard-filled ramekins. Place ramekins in a deep roasting pan.

3 Pour boiling water into the roasting pan to three-quarters of the way up the sides of the ramekins. Bake the custards for 40 minutes. Serve warm or cold with the pulp and seeds from the remaining passion fruit spooned over the top.

oriental fruit salad

ingredients

3 stalks lemon grass
60 g (2 oz) superfine sugar
1 small rock melon (cantaloupe)
1 mango
425 g (14 oz) can lychees, drained
fresh mint leaves to garnish
serves 4

preparation time
30 minutes,
plus 20 minutes
cooling and 30
minutes chilling

cooking time
5 minutes

**nutritional value
per serve**
fat: 0.2 g
carbohydrate: 13 g
protein: 0.7 g

1 Peel the outer layers from the lemon grass stalks and finely chop the lower white bulbous parts. In a pan, place the lemon grass, sugar and 100 ml (3½ fl oz) water. Simmer, stirring, for 5 minutes or until sugar dissolves, then bring to the boil. Remove from heat and leave to cool for 20 minutes. Refrigerate for 30 minutes.

2 Halve the melon and scrape out the seeds. Cut into wedges, remove skin and cut the flesh into small chunks. Slice off the two fat sides of the mango close to the stone. Cut a criss-cross pattern across the flesh, of each piece, then push the skin up to

expose the cubes of flesh and cut them off. Place the melon, mango and lychees in serving bowls. Strain the lemon grass syrup and pour over the fruit. Decorate with mint.

glossary

al dente: Italian term to describe pasta and rice that are cooked until tender but still firm to the bite.

bake blind: to bake pastry shells without their fillings. Line the raw pastry shell with wax paper and fill with raw rice or dried beans to prevent collapsed sides and puffed bottom. Remove paper and fill 5 minutes before completion of cooking time.

baste: to spoon hot cooking liquid over food at intervals during cooking to moisten and flavor it.

beat: to make a mixture smooth with rapid and regular motions using a spatula, wire whisk or electric mixer; to make a mixture light and smooth by enclosing air.

beurre manié: equal quantities of butter and flour mixed together to a smooth paste and stirred bit by bit into a soup, stew or sauce while on the heat to thicken. Stop adding when desired thickness results.

bind: to add egg or a thick sauce to hold ingredients together when cooked.

blanch: to plunge some foods into boiling water for less than a minute and immediately plunge into iced water. This is to brighten the color of some vegetables; to remove skin from tomatoes and nuts.

blend: to mix 2 or more ingredients thoroughly together; do not confuse with blending in an electric blender.

boil: to cook in a liquid brought to boiling point and kept there.

boiling point: when bubbles rise continually and break over the entire surface of the liquid, reaching a temperature of 100°C (212°F). In some cases food is held at this high temperature for a few seconds then heat is turned to low for slower cooking. See simmer.

bouquet garni: a bundle of several herbs tied together with string for easy removal, placed into pots of stock, soups and stews for flavor. A few sprigs of fresh thyme, parsley and bay leaf are used. Can be purchased in sachet form for convenience.

caramelize: to heat sugar in a heavy-bottomed pan until it liquefies and develops a caramel color. Vegetables such as blanched carrots and sautéed onions may be sprinkled with sugar and caramelized.

chill: to place in the refrigerator or stir over ice until cold.

clarify: to make a liquid clear by removing sediments and impurities. To melt fat and remove any sediment.

coat: to dust or roll food items in flour to cover the surface before the food is cooked. Also, to coat in flour, egg and breadcrumbs.

cool: to stand at room temperature until some or all heat is removed, e.g., cool a little, cool completely.

cream: to make creamy and fluffy by working the mixture with the back of a wooden spoon, usually refers to creaming butter and sugar or margarine. May also be creamed with an electric mixer.

croutons: small cubes of bread, toasted or fried, used as an addition to salads or as a garnish to soups and stews.

crudite: raw vegetable sticks served with a dipping sauce.

crumb: to coat foods in flour, egg and breadcrumbs to form a protective coating for foods that are fried. Also adds flavor, texture and enhances appearance.

cube: to cut into small pieces with six even sides, e.g., cubes of meat.

cut in: to combine fat and flour using 2 knives scissor fashion or with a pastry blender, to make pastry.

deglaze: to dissolve dried out cooking juices left on the bottom and sides of a roasting pan or skillet. Add a little water, wine or stock, scrape and stir over heat until dissolved. Resulting liquid is used to make a flavorsome gravy or added to a sauce or casserole.

degrease: to skim fat from the surface of cooking liquids, e.g., stocks, soups, casseroles.

dice: to cut into small cubes.

dredge: to heavily coat with confectioners' sugar, sugar, flour or cornstarch.

dressing: a mixture added to completed dishes to add moisture and flavor, e.g., salads, cooked vegetables.

drizzle: to pour in a fine thread-like stream moving over a surface.

egg wash: beaten egg with milk or water used to brush over pastry, bread dough or cookies to give a sheen and golden brown color.

essence: a strong flavoring liquid, usually made by distillation. Only a few drops are needed to flavor.

fillet: a piece of prime meat, fish or poultry that is boneless or has all bones removed.

flake: to separate cooked fish into flakes, removing any bones and skin, using 2 forks.

flame: to ignite warmed alcohol over food or to pour into a skillet with food, ignite then serve.

flute: to make decorative indentations around the pastry rim before baking.

fold in: combining of a light, whipped or creamed mixture with other ingredients. Add a portion of the other ingredients at a time and mix using a gentle circular motion, over and under the mixture so that air will not be lost. Use a silver spoon or spatula.

glaze: to brush or coat food with a liquid that will give the finished product a glossy appearance, and on baked products, a golden brown color.

grease: to rub the surface of a metal or heatproof pan with oil or fat, to prevent the food from sticking.

herbed butter: softened butter mixed with minced fresh herbs and re-chilled. Used to serve on grilled meats and fish.

hors d'ouvre: small savory foods served as an appetizer, popularly known today as 'finger food'.

infuse: to steep foods in a liquid until the liquid absorbs their flavour.

joint: to cut poultry and game into serving pieces by dividing at the joint.

julienne: to cut some food, e.g., vegetables and processed meats into fine strips the length of matchsticks. Used for inclusion in salads or as a garnish to cooked dishes.

knead: to work a yeast dough in a pressing, stretching and folding motion with the heel of the hand until smooth and elastic to develop the gluten strands. Non-yeast doughs should be lightly and quickly handled as gluten development is not desired.

line: to cover the inside of a baking pan with paper for the easy removal of the cooked product from the baking pan.

macerate: to stand fruit in a syrup, liqueur or spirit to give added flavor.

marinade: a flavored liquid, into which food is placed for some time to give it flavor and to tenderize. Marinades include an acid ingredient such as vinegar or wine, oil and seasonings.

mask: to evenly cover cooked food portions with a sauce, mayonnaise or savory jelly.

pan-fry: to fry foods in a small amount of fat or oil, sufficient to coat the bottom of the pan or skillet.

parboil: to boil until partially cooked. The food is then finished by some other method.

pare: to peel the skin from vegetables and fruit. Peel is the popular term but pare is the name given to the knife used; paring knife.

pith: the white lining between the zest and flesh of oranges, grapefruit and lemons.

pit: to remove stones or seeds from olives, cherries, dates.

pitted: the olives, cherries, dates, etc., with the stone removed, e.g., purchase pitted dates.

poach: to simmer gently in enough hot liquid to almost cover the food so shape will be retained.

pound: to flatten meats with a meat mallet; to reduce to a paste or small particles with a mortar and pestle.

simmer: to cook in liquid just below boiling point at about 96°C (205°F) with small bubbles rising gently to the surface.

skim: to remove fat or froth from the surface of simmering food.

stock: the liquid produced when meat, poultry, fish or vegetables have been simmered in water to extract the flavor. Used as a base for soups, sauces, casseroles, etc. Convenience stock products are available.

sweat: to cook sliced onions or vegetables, in a small amount of butter in a covered pan over low heat, to soften them and release flavor without coloring.

conversions

measurements differ from country to country, so it's important to understand what the differences are. This Measurements Guide gives you simple "at-a-glance" information for using the recipes in this book, wherever you may be.

Cooking is not an exact science – minor variations in measurements won't make a difference to your cooking.

equipment

There is a difference in the size of measuring cups used internationally, but the difference is minimal (only 2–3 teaspoons). We use the Australian standard metric measurements in our recipes:

1 teaspoon ....5 ml	1 tablespoon....20 ml
1/2 cup......125 ml	1 cup.....250 ml
4 cups...1 liter	

Measuring cups come in sets of one cup (250 ml), 1/2 cup (125 ml), 1/3 cup (80 ml) and 1/4 cup (60 ml). Use these for measuring liquids and certain dry ingredients.
Measuring spoons come in a set of four and should be used for measuring dry and liquid ingredients.
When using cup or spoon measures always make them level (unless the recipe indicates otherwise).

dry versus wet ingredients

While this system of measures is consistent for liquids, it's more difficult to quantify dry ingredients. For instance, one level cup equals: 200 g of light brown sugar; 210 g of superfine sugar; and 110 g of confectioners' sugar.

When measuring dry ingredients such as flour, don't push the flour down or shake it into the cup. It is best just to spoon the flour in until it reaches the desired amount. When measuring liquids use a clear vessel indicating metric levels.

Always use medium eggs (55–60 g) when eggs are required in a recipe.

dry

metric (grams)	imperial (ounces)
30 g	1 oz
60 g	2 oz
90 g	3 oz
100 g	3 1/2 oz
125 g	4 oz
150 g	5 oz
185 g	6 oz
200 g	7 oz
250 g	8 oz
280 g	9 oz
315 g	10 oz
330 g	11 oz
370 g	12 oz
400 g	13 oz
440 g	14 oz
470 g	15 oz
500 g	16 oz (1 lb)
750 g	24 oz (1 1/2 lb)
1000 g (1 kg)	32 oz (2 lb)

liquids

metric (milliliters)	imperial (fluid ounces)
30 ml	1 fl oz
60 ml	2 fl oz
90 ml	3 fl oz
100 ml	3 1/2 fl oz
125 ml	4 fl oz
150 ml	5 fl oz
190 ml	6 fl oz
250 ml	8 fl oz
300 ml	10 fl oz
500 ml	16 fl oz (1 pint)
600 ml	20 fl oz
1000 ml (1 liter)	32 fl oz

oven

Your oven should always be at the right temperature before placing the food in it to be cooked. Note that if your oven doesn't have a fan you may need to cook food for a little longer.

microwave

It is difficult to give an exact cooking time for microwave cooking. It is best to watch what you are cooking closely to monitor its progress.

standing time

Many foods continue to cook when you take them out of the oven or microwave. If a recipe states that the food needs to "stand" after cooking, be sure not to overcook the dish.

can sizes

The can sizes available in your supermarket or grocery store may not be the same as specified in the recipe. Don't worry if there is a small variation in size—it's unlikely to make a difference to the end result.

cooking temperatures	°C (celsius)	°F (fahrenheit)	gas mark
very slow	120	250	1/2
slow	150	300	2
moderately slow	160	315	2-3
moderate	180	350	4
moderate hot	190	375	5
	200	400	6
hot	220	425	7
very hot	230	450	8
	240	475	9
	250	500	10

index